Jools Holl

The Hand That Changed It ...nd

Congratulations on buying this book. Thank you for taking an interest in some of the music I have written. When I first started to play the piano I learnt by ear. My big jump forward was when I learnt what chords were. George Harrison once told me that The Beatles, in their early teens, got the bus to Wallasey to see a man who could show them the chord of B7, and after this they never looked back. I learnt a great deal from looking at the songbooks of The Beatles and Tamla Motown and The Rolling Stones as I was growing up. Some of the pieces in this book are written out with chords like those early books I looked at. For the more advanced some of my piano pieces have been transcribed. Please feel free to add your own elements, feel and improvisation. Finally, I hope this book may be especially helpful to people who can't quite see over the top of the piano, as it may be usefully placed upon the stool raising the pianist's height and improving his view. Music can be an endless journey of discovery and pleasure. You have my best wishes for enjoying it.

Jools Holland

Published 2004

Arrangements by Phil Veacock
Engraving by Artemis Music Limited
Cover Photograph by Kevin Westenberg
Photographs on pages 2 and 3 courtesy of Jools Holland

Some of my co-writers and collaborators.

Self and a bunch of 'Chrissies'.

Contents

Bloodsucker Blues

Words and Music by Jools Holland, Christopher Holland and Richard Holland

All That You Are

Words and Music by Jools Holland and Eric Bibb

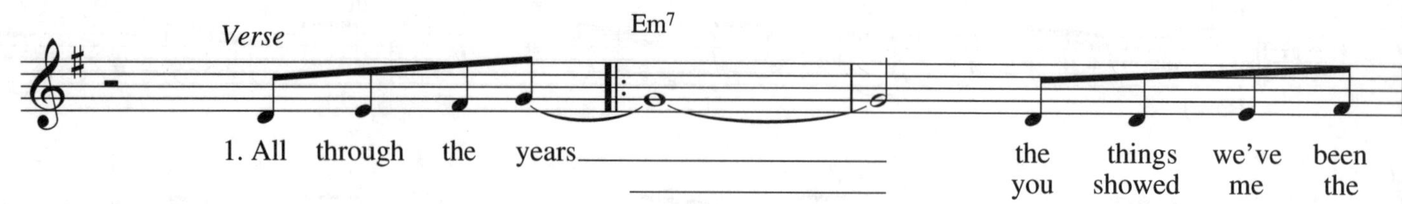

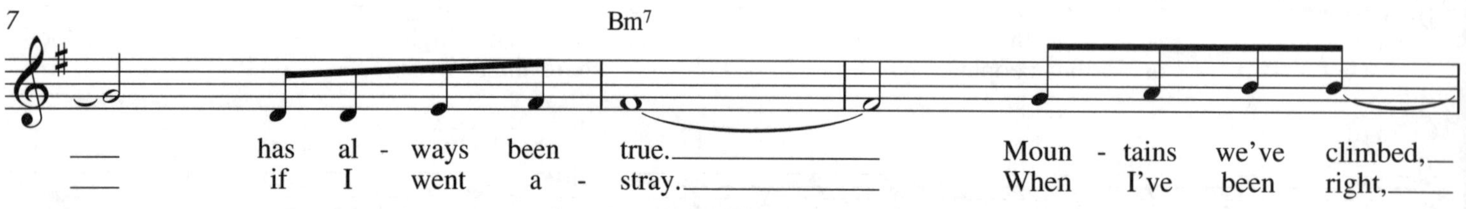

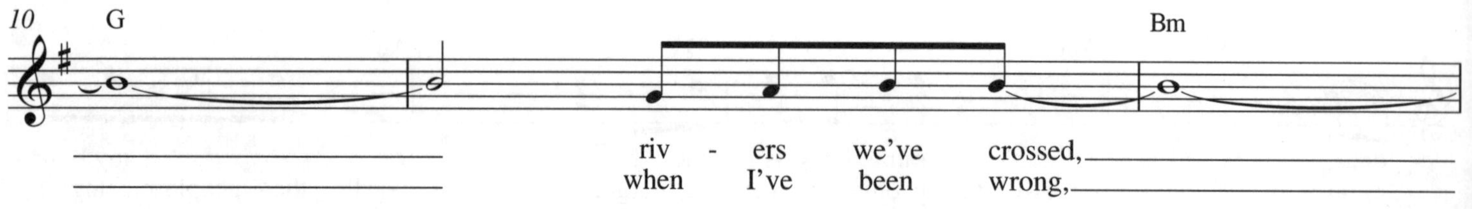

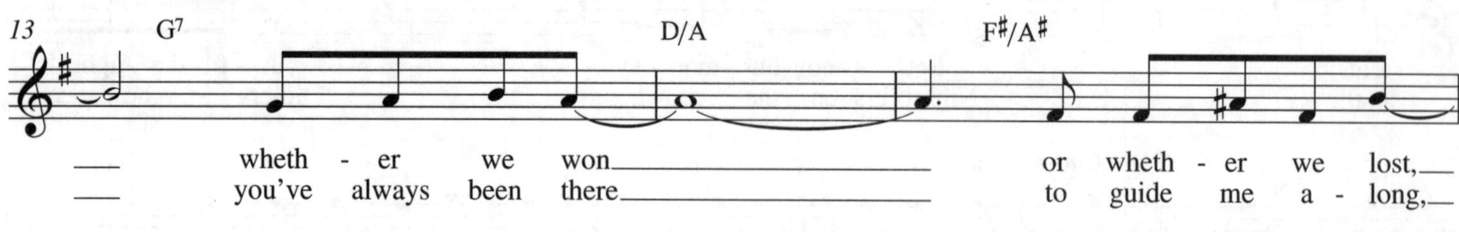

19
F♯/A♯
Bm7
A/C♯
proud and true
to the faith in my heart
22
D
F♯/A♯
Bm7
that's what you taught me to do.
25
G6
G6
B7/F♯
You didn't have to preach it
your act - ions would teach
28
Em
Em
D/A
it;
with all of my heart
I want to
31
G♯o
G/A
D
Fine
1.
thank you for all that you are.
2. When I was con - fused
34
2.
Bridge
G
I learned how to give,
how to be true;
37
A♭o
D/A
I learned how to live,
liv -
40
F♯/A♯
Bm
G6
D. 𝄋 al Fine
- ving with you.
Stand

Brick Lane

Music by Jools Holland

17
C/G
G
C6/G
G
21
D7
26
sim.
30
34

38
41
44
47
50
trem.

53
56
60
64
69
8va
rall.
8vb

Dr Jazz

Words and Music by Jools Holland

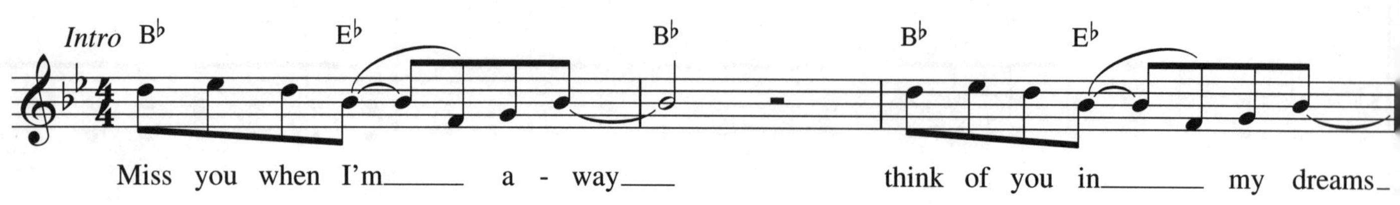

Intro
B♭
E♭
B♭
B♭
E♭
Miss you when I'm a - way
think of you in my dreams

4
B♭
F7
you're the one that I love
that's the

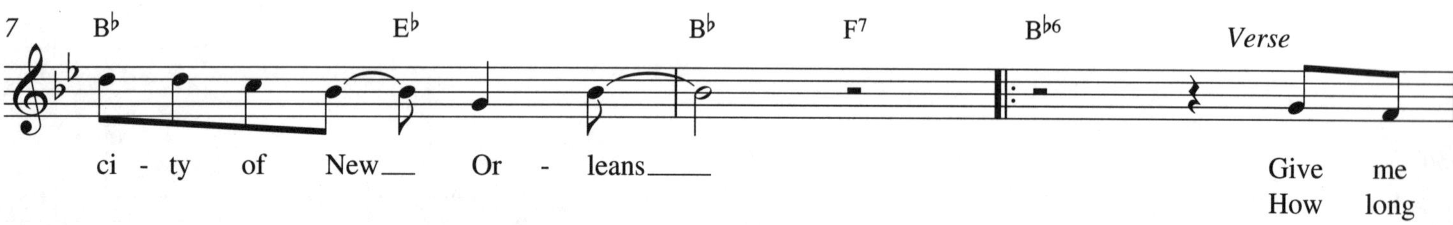

7
B♭
E♭
B♭
F7
B♭6
Verse
ci - ty of New Or - leans
Give me
How long

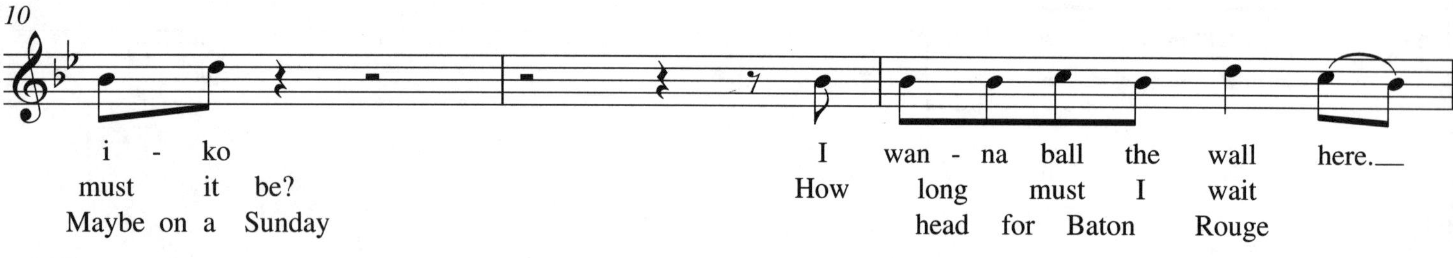

10
i - ko
must it be?
Maybe on a Sunday
I wan - na ball the wall here.
How long must I wait
head for Baton Rouge

13
F7
B♭6
Shuf - fle in Du Maine
til High - way 49
Dancing with a Cajun

16
hear the hoo - ka cum - by.
takes me to your gate?
twisting a - way my blues.
Meet my tip - i - ti - na
I eat a bowl of gum - bo
Then a drop of rain

19
F7
love and hold her tight - ly. I
that Creole child will serve,
trickle on my eyes as
22
B♭6
wan - na see her sway - ing New Or - le - ans night - ly.
sit on the veranda happy in a Dixie world.
I look up and smile at the rhythm that never never
25
F7
B♭
I wan - na be the - re.
Backing vocals: Drink - ing in the morn - ing
dies.
28
F7
F
Doc - tor Jazz, Doc - tor Jazz, make my jel - ly roll, you
hol - ler in the eve - ning.
31
Gm
E°
Chorus
B♭
quick - en my pulse, you make my rhy - thm slow. Craw - fish gum - bo,
34
F
B♭
E♭
Edim
rhy - thm from the jun - gle, big chief rock - ing, fol - low the voo - doo king.
37
B♭/F
F
B♭
3rd time repeat ad lib. to Fine
Oo - la mol - la wal - la dol - la that's what the 'Fes' he sing.

From Grey To Blue

Words and Music by Jools Holland

F7
B♭
Verse
B♭Δ
1. You're too far from
2. Just a phone call or

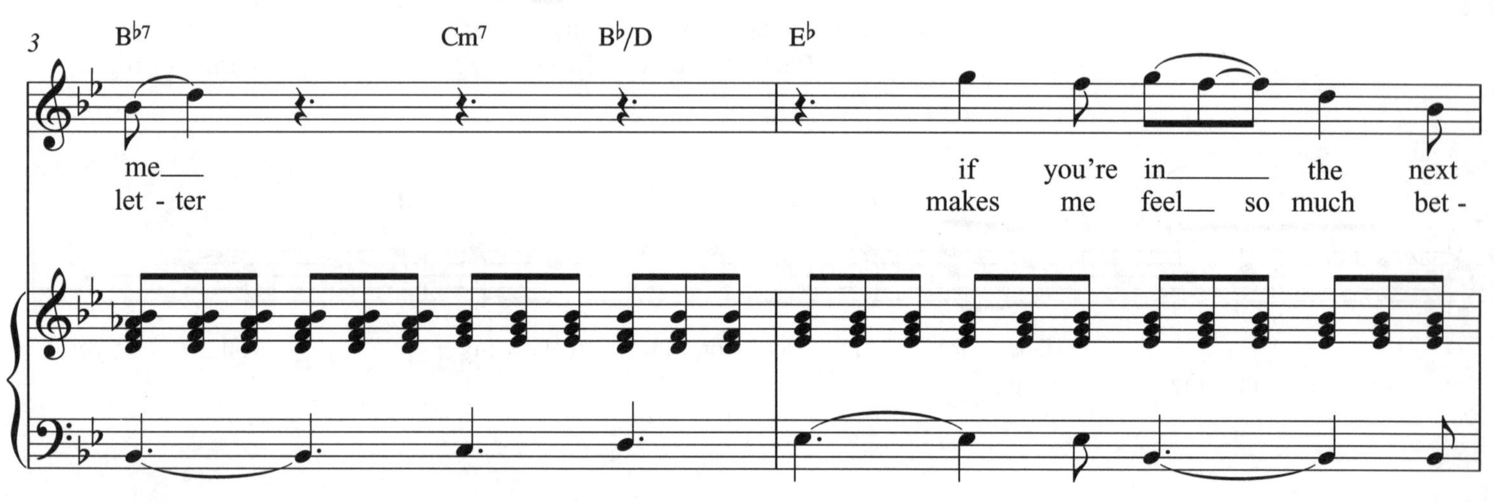
3
B♭7
Cm7
B♭/D
E♭
me
let - ter
if you're in the next
makes me feel so much bet -

5
E♭m/A♭
B♭
Dm
Gm
room.
-ter.
From grey to blue

To Coda last time
E♭
F
B♭
E♭
I'm miss - ing you.
1.
2.
B♭/D
Cm
F7
B♭/D
Cm
B♭7/D
E♭
Bridge
F7
And now you've gone
or 8vb
B♭
Gm
I'll think of you

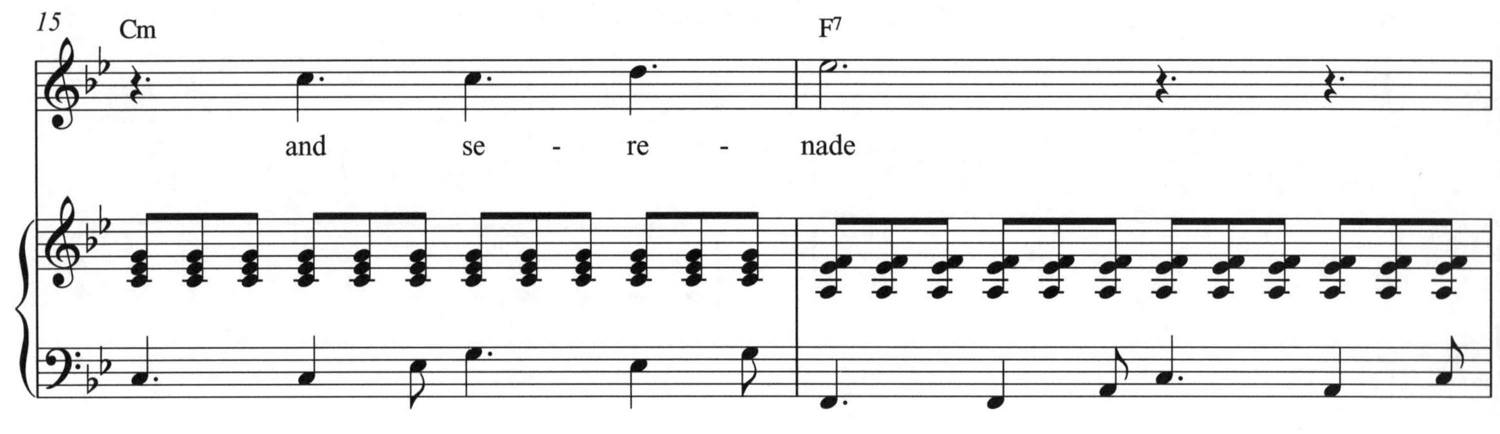
15
Cm
F7
and se - re - nade

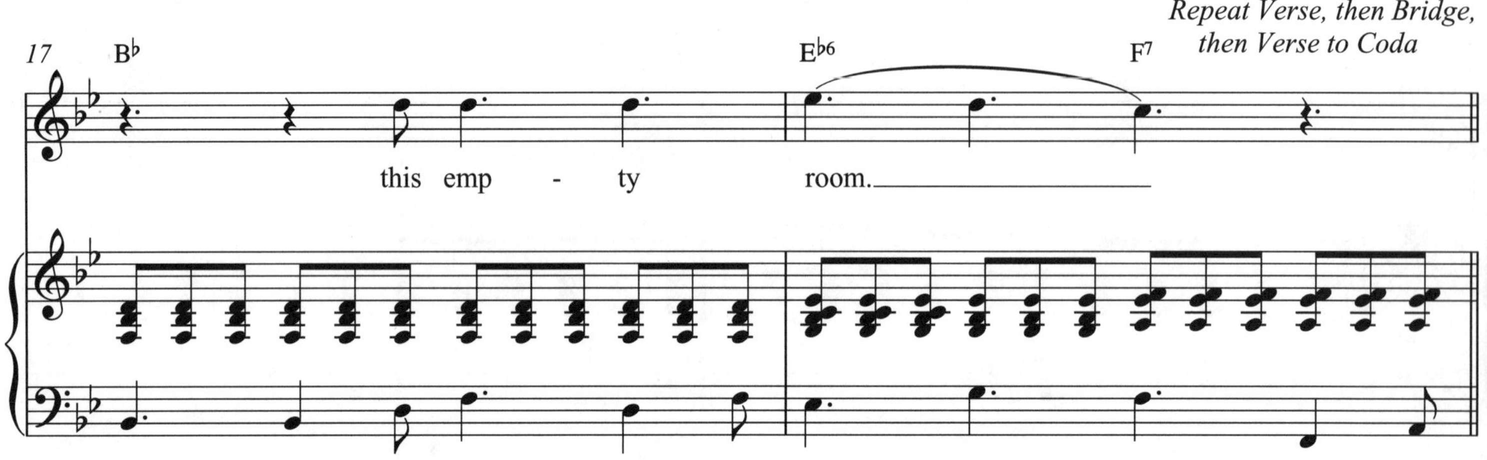
Repeat Verse, then Bridge, then Verse to Coda
17
B♭
E♭6
F7
this emp - ty room.

CODA
19
N.C.
B7
B♭9
you.
out of tempo
8va
L.H.

3. Miss your smiling eyes
You know you're my paradise
From grey to blue
I'm missing you.

4. As we waltz upon the carpet
Of love's caravan
From grey to blue
I'm missing you.

Out Of This World

Words and Music by Jools Holland, Sam Brown and Chrissie Hynde

The Hand That Changed Its Mind

Words and Music by Jools Holland and Mac Rebennack

Spoken: Need a helpin' hand coz my mind underhanded me.
Way down the line on the sands of time.
Keep it dissatisfied with your back hand signs.
Got a hand but my hand dun changed its mind.

It's So Blue

Words and Music by Jools Holland, Christopher Holland, Richard Holland and Paul Carrack

25 C/B♭ Dm C/E F G9 Dm C/E F G9 C *Chorus* C C9/E

on your sheets in your room.___ It's so

29 F G9 C C C C7/E

blue this af - ter - noon. I'll come to

33 F G9 C C C7/E

you, I'll be there soon. It's so

37 F G9 C G/B Am C7/E

blue this af - ter - noon. I'll come to

41 F G9 C (F/C) 1. C

you, I'll be there soon.

45 2. Am Fm/A♭ C/G F6 *Vocal ad lib.* Am Fm/A♭

I'll be there soon yes_ I will.___

Repeat Chorus to end

June Rose Lane

Words and Music by Jools Holland

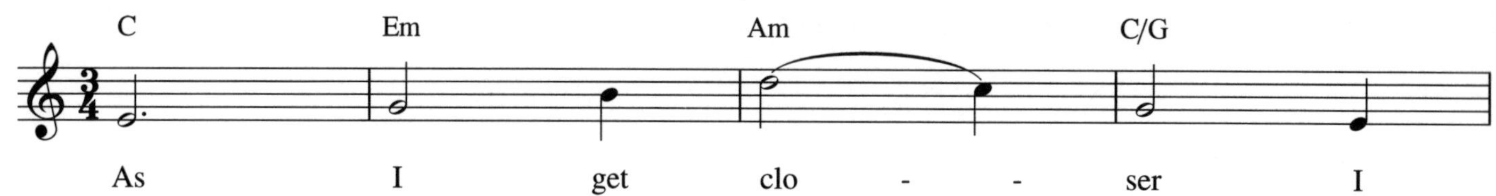
C
Em
Am
C/G
As I get clo - - ser I

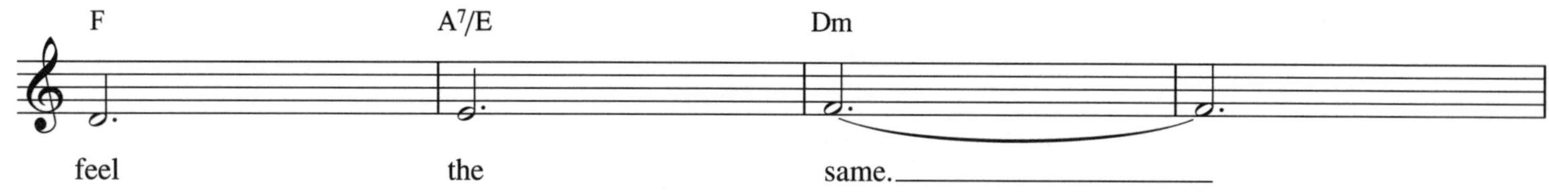
F
A7/E
Dm
feel the same.

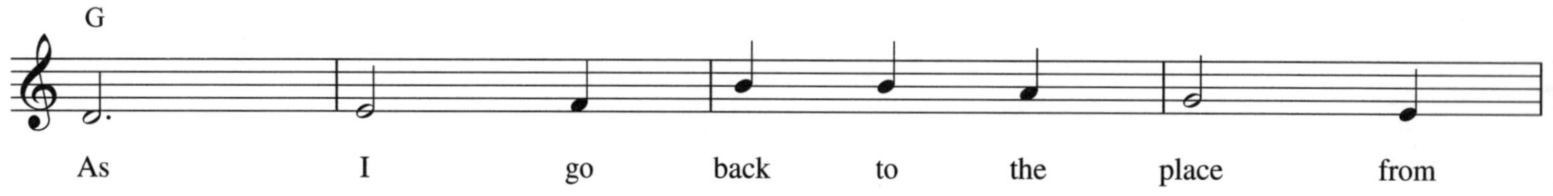
G
As I go back to the place from

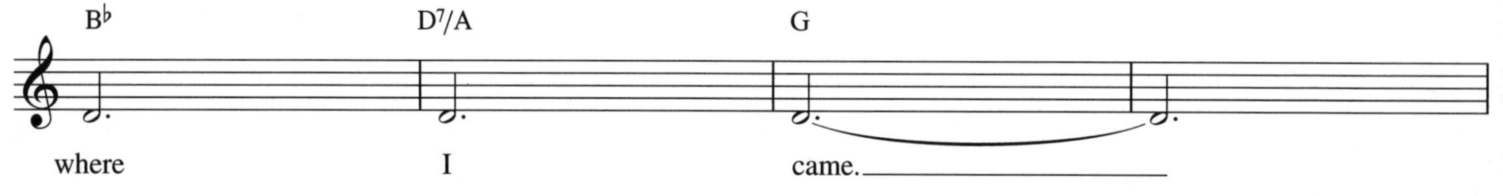
B♭
D7/A
G
where I came.

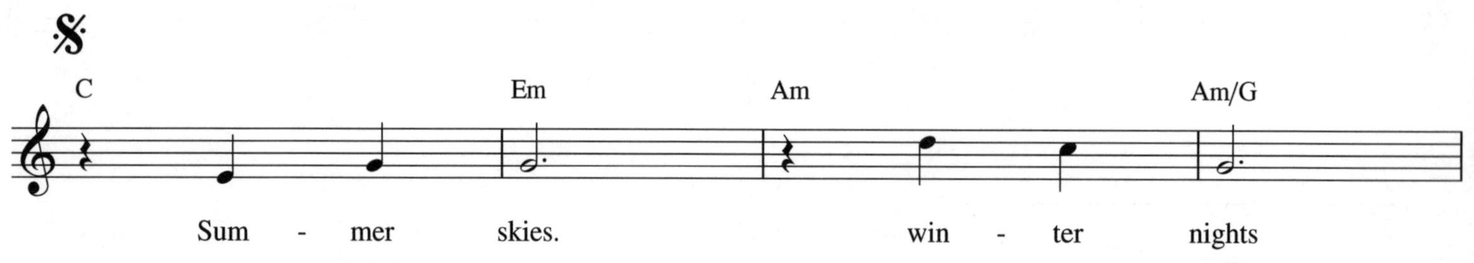
C
Em
Am
Am/G
Sum - mer skies. win - ter nights

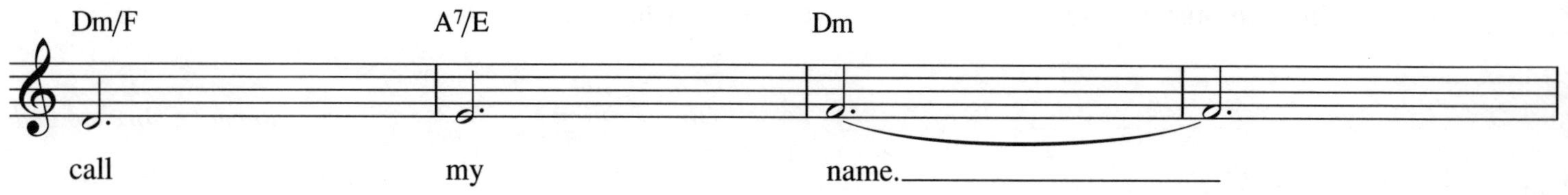
Dm/F
A7/E
Dm
call my name.

Cdim/E♭
C/G
Am
I'm
go - - ing
home
to

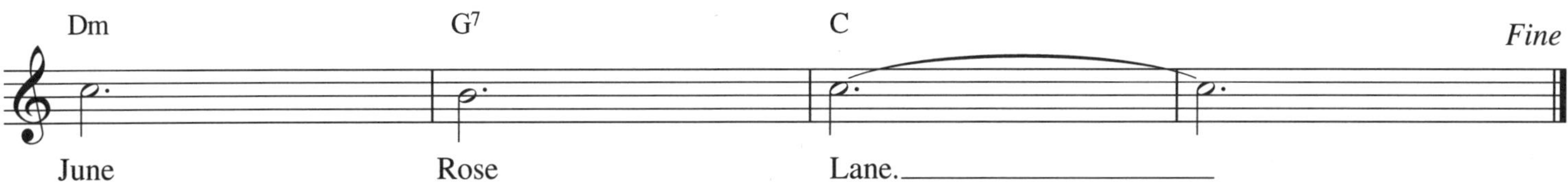
Dm
G7
C
Fine
June
Rose
Lane.

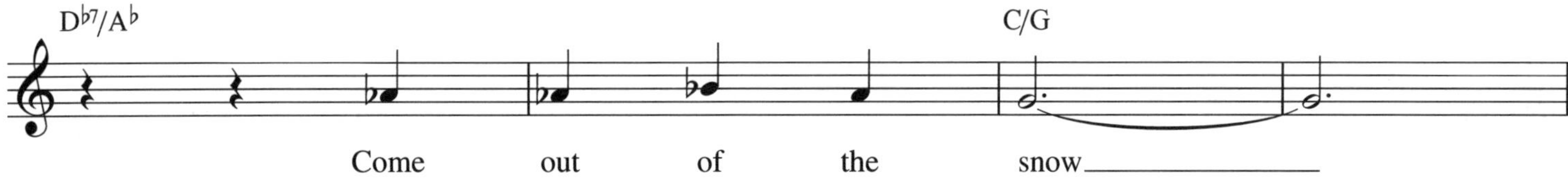
D♭7/A♭
C/G
Come
out
of
the
snow

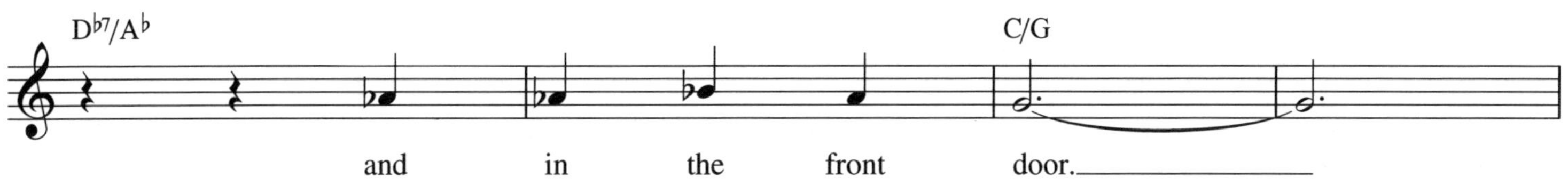
D♭7/A♭
C/G
and
in
the
front
door.

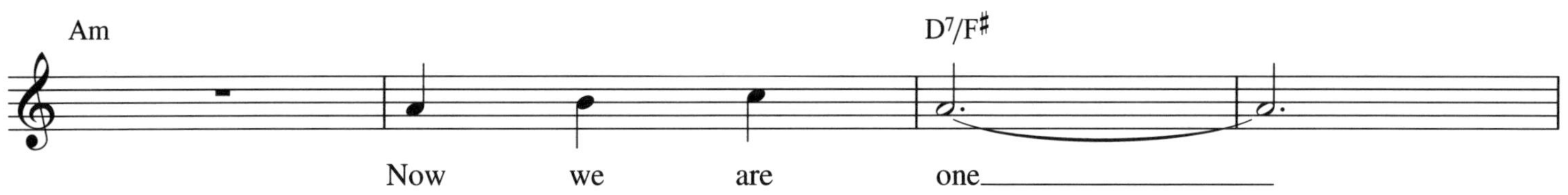
Am
D7/F♯
Now
we
are
one

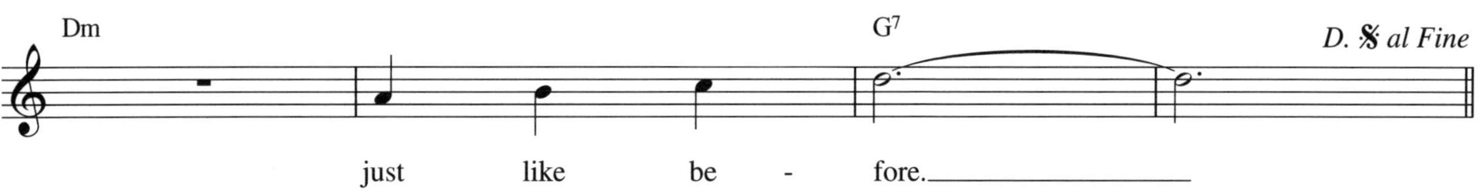
Dm
G7
D. 𝄋 al Fine
just
like
be - fore.

2. Toast with me to the days we spent
In the arms of other men's wives
The days we spent in our mother's arms
Are the happiest days of our lives.

Oranges And Lemons Again

Words and Music by Jools Holland and Suggs
(Ska) Intro
It's the crook - ed leg, the crook - ed mile, the ho - tel lift and the me - nac - ing smile. The en - er - gy of an i - ti - ne - rant child to catch a glimpse of Mis - ter Os - car Wilde.
And it's sweet Gene Vincent, mean old Ronnie Kray, the low slung slouch of the bird of prey. Trouser pocket boys in un - romantic places, cigarettes falling from their sallow faces. He's
And they're lurking in the doorway of every town, rough kids rally with their sorrow drowned. Burnt out faces and their ash - tray eyes, when up goes the cry through the perforated sky. He's
1st time only

19 C Am C
Wa - ter - borne South - end on Sea, twist - ed bend this a -
22 Am C
- bi - li - ty, Lord Up - min - ster, Bo Didd - ly and
24 Am C
Rich - ard the Third, with the most un - roy - al mouth that you've
26 Am B♭
ev - er heard. He's nev - er gon - na do it? Oh he
28 F G
has an' all! They're smil - in' po - lite - ly but they're
30 G7 Chorus C C/E
real - ly ap - palled. And it's turned out o - ran - ges and
32 F G C C/E F G
le - mons a - gain, all three bells in a row. We're
3rd time repeat Chorus to fade
35 C C/E F G (unis) G7
in and out The Ea - gle and up and down the Ci - ty Road.

Panic Attack

Music by Jools Holland

13
3
16
19
C
22
G
25
D7
1.
G

2.
G

45
48
3
51
54
C
57
G

60
D7
1.
G
64
2.
68
ff
71
C
G
74
D7
1.

77
G
2.
80
3
G
83
86
B♭/B♮
Am/C G/D
89
E♭/E♮
Dm/F C/G
B♭
Am
Gm
C6
G
A♭7
G

Return Of The Blues Cowboy

Words and Music by Jools Holland and Joe Strummer

2. Well well I tell nobody was pleased to see him back
When he kicked in the snug saloon door.
Albeit he misjudged the swing and he kicked himself onto the floor.
Yeah, there sure was a mixed reception, to the comeback of the blues cowboy
From way outta, from way outta nineteen hundred and forty four.

3. But now somehow he's loose on the streets.
In all Chicago you can't lock no coop-house door.
Oh, I'm seeing the alleys slink with guitar slingers who just don't want to sling no more.
Don't hold your breath baby, but it's the return of the blues cowboy
From way back before nineteen hundred and forty four.

D. 𝄋 You can pick at the rockface baby,
You'll find a bead of sweat in every pore.

Snowflake Boogie

Words and Music by Jools Holland

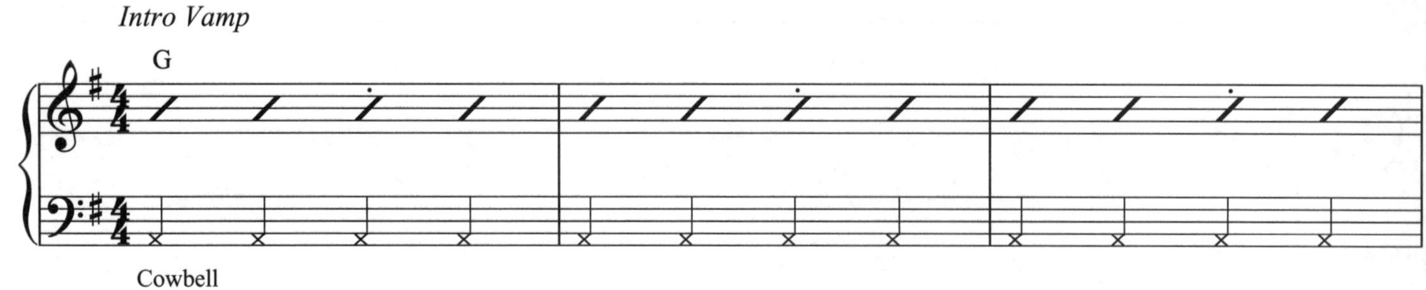

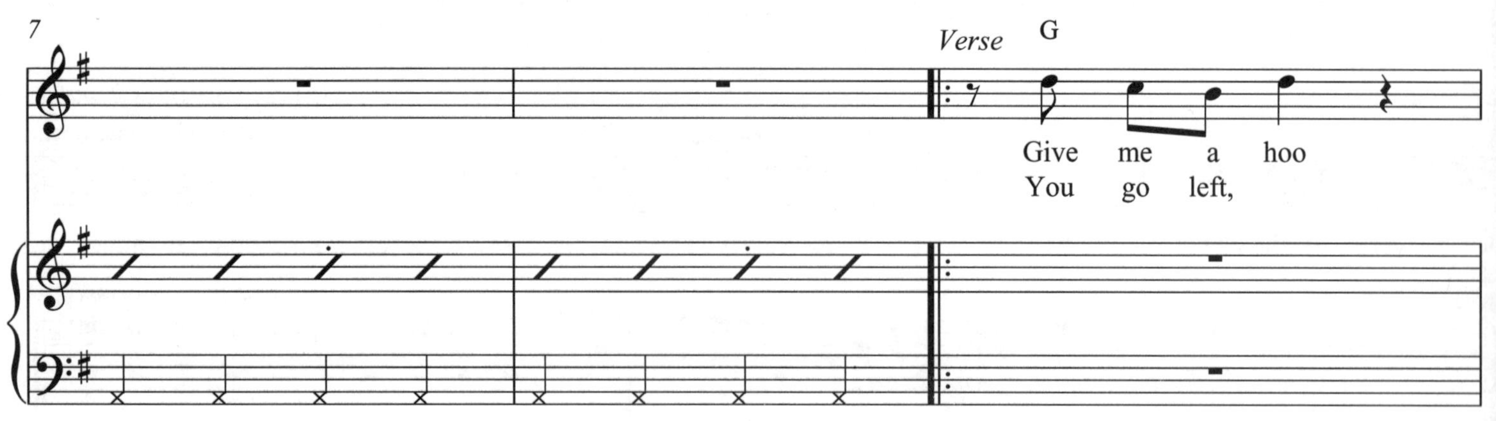

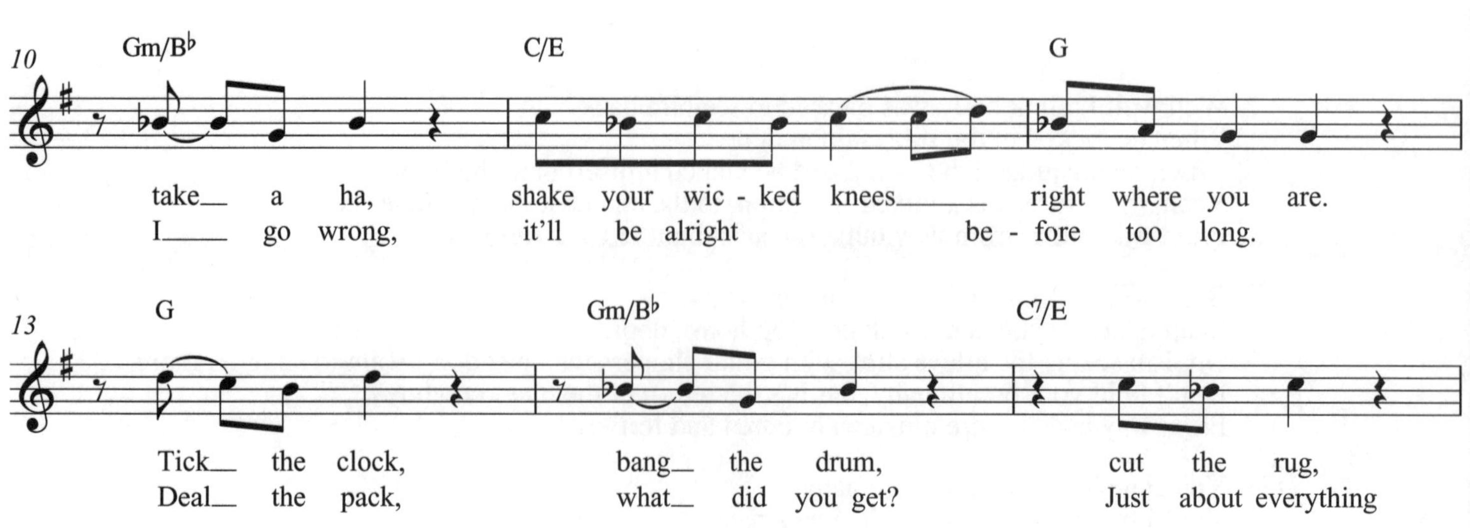

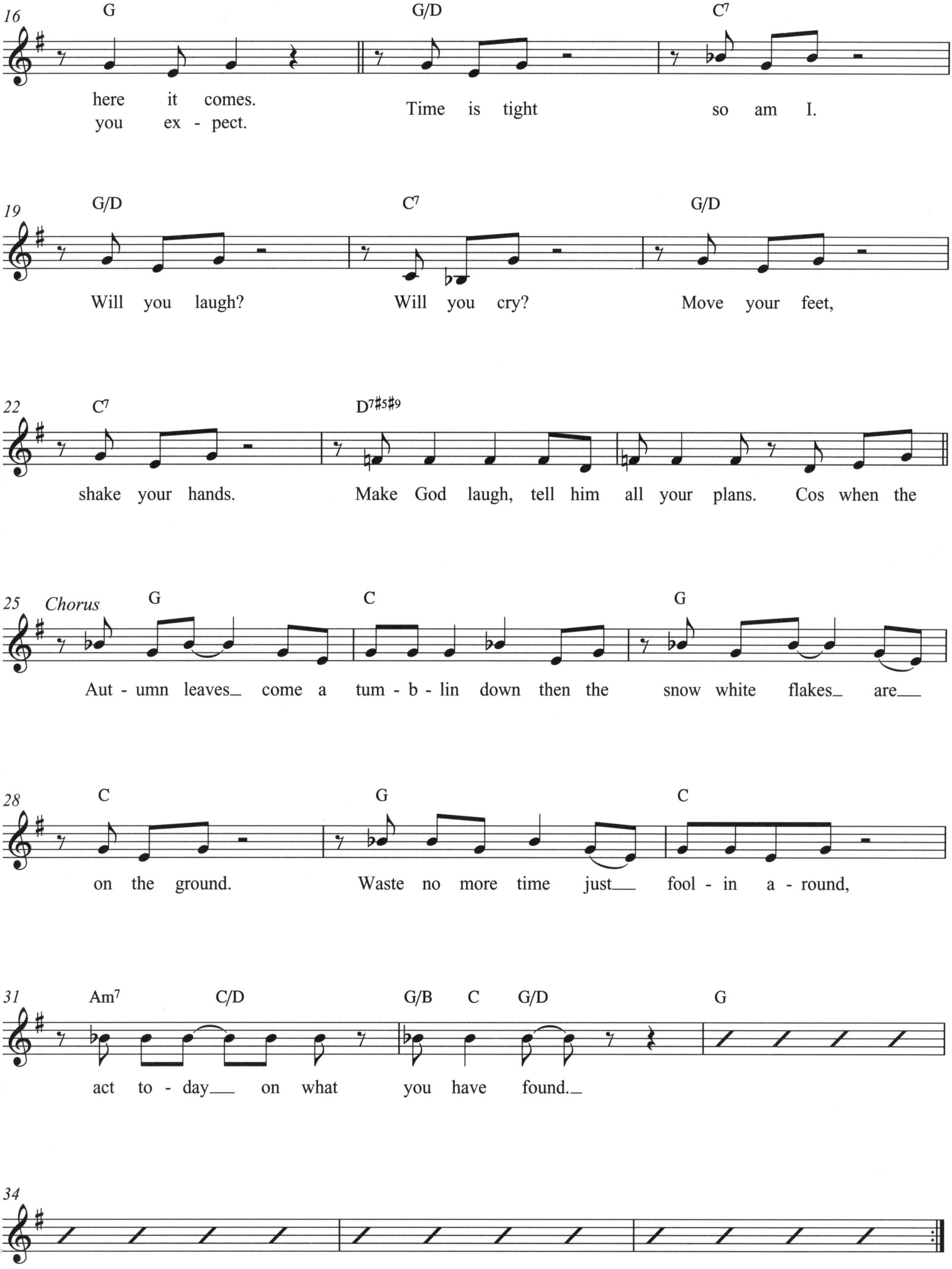

16
G
G/D
C7
here it comes.
you ex - pect.
Time is tight
so am I.
19
G/D
C7
G/D
Will you laugh?
Will you cry?
Move your feet,
22
C7
D7#5#9
shake your hands.
Make God laugh, tell him all your plans. Cos when the
25 Chorus
G
C
G
Aut - umn leaves come a tum - b - lin down then the snow white flakes are
28
C
G
C
on the ground.
Waste no more time just fool - in a - round,
31
Am7
C/D
G/B
C
G/D
G
act to - day on what you have found.
34

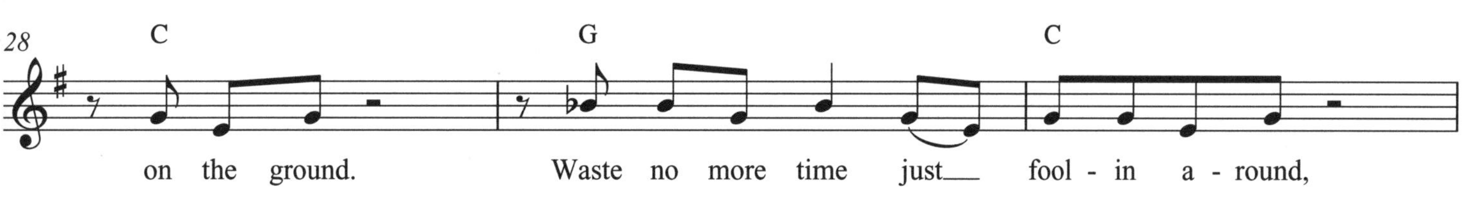

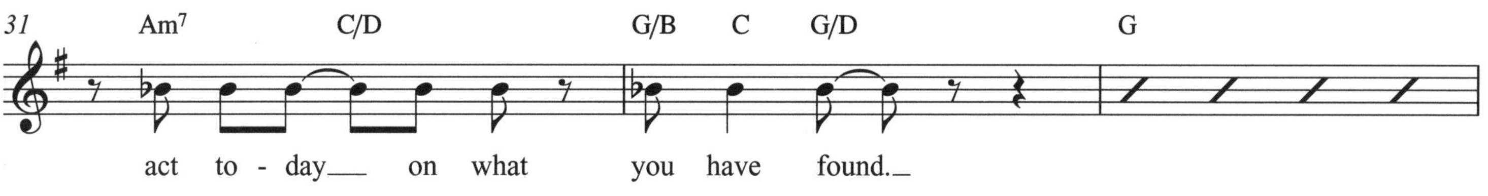

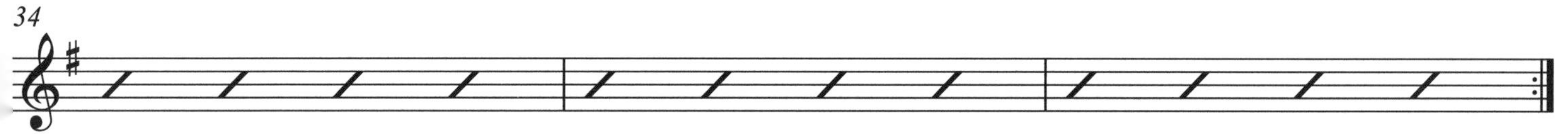

Temple Bar

Music by Jools Holland

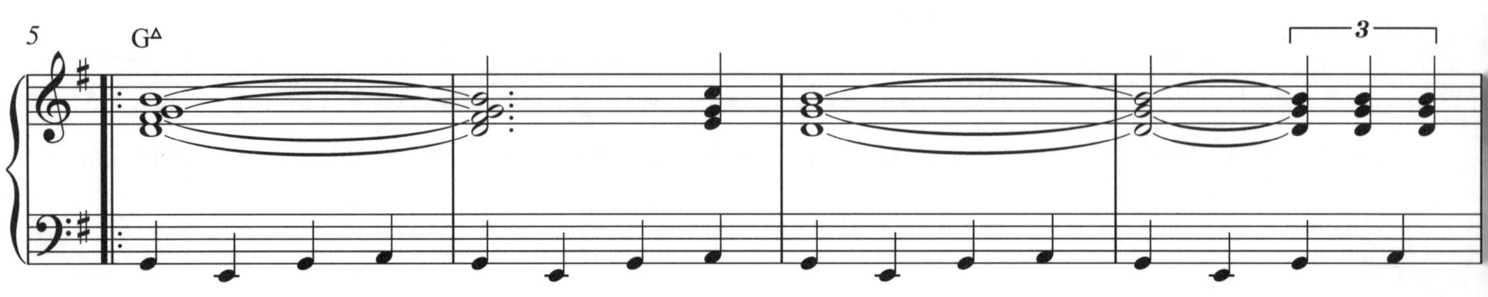

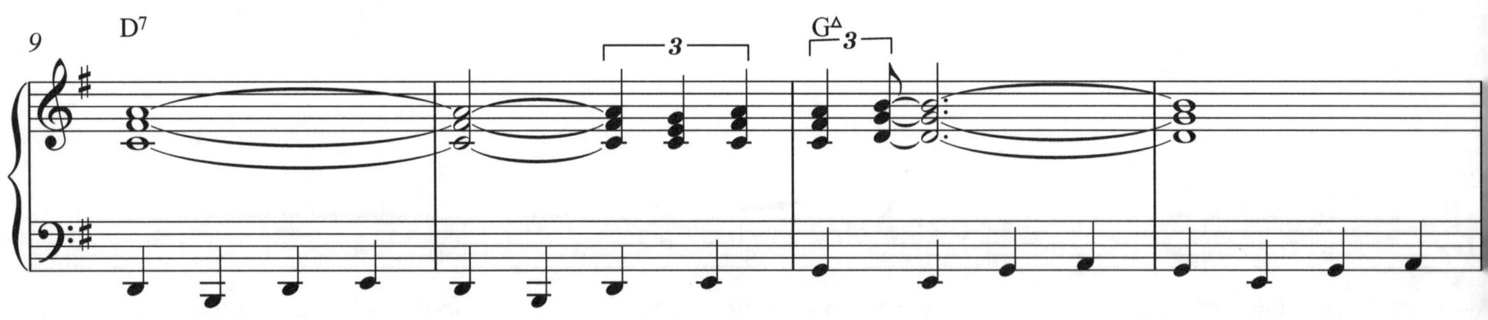

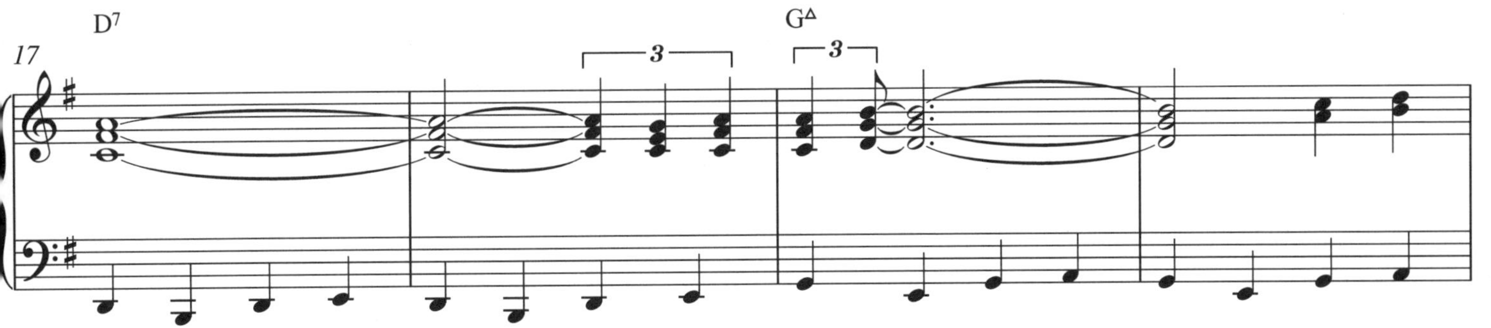
D7
G△
17
3
3

21
C
G
3
3

25
Am7
G
3

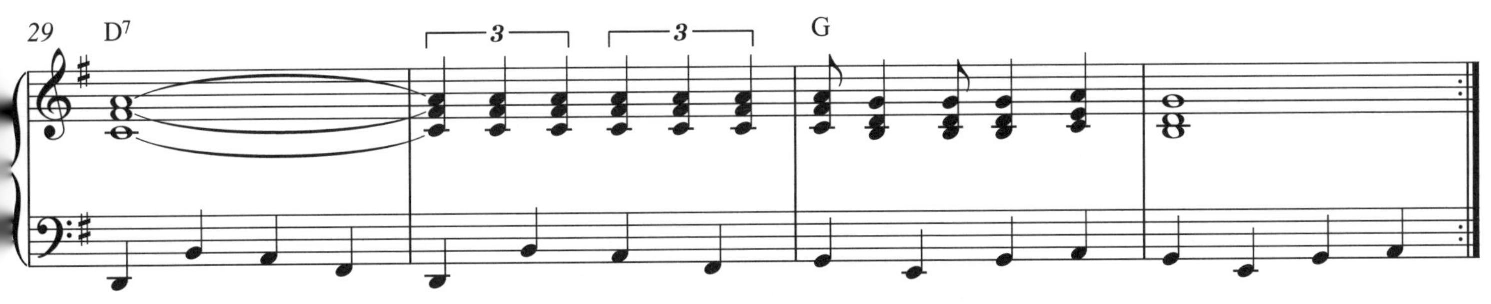
29
D7
G
3
3

Together We Are Strong

Words and Music by Jools Holland and Sam Brown

Town And Country Rhythm And Blues

Words and Music by Jools Holland and Chris Difford

29 E♭/F
B♭/F
I love my life,
well it's all right.
33 E♭/F
D7
When I'm not here
I'm not all there.
37 Bm♭5 Chorus
E7(♯5) E7
Am7(♭5)
Town and coun - try rhy - thm and blues
al - ways makes me
40 D7(♯5) D7
Bm7(♭5)
E7(♯5) E7
think of you.
Head - ing out in my walk - ing shoes
43 Am7(♭5)
D7(♯5) D7
Gm7 (Bass)
town and coun - try rhy - thm and blues.
46
Gm7
3. Well I ride my bike,
50
I drive my car.
The sun is burn - ing
54
Cm7
but I won't go far
with - out the speed;

58
Gm7
that's all I need to get where I'm go - ing
62
Am
from where I've been. Town and coun - try
67
Em
rhy - thm and blues. It's big tall build - ings,
71
E♭/F
it's per - fect views. I love my life,
75
B♭
E♭/F
well it's all right. When I'm not here
79
D7
Bm♭5
E7(♯5)
E7
I'm not all there. Town and coun - try rhy - thm and blues
83
Am7(♭5)
D7(♯5)
D7
Bm7(♭5)
al - ways makes me think of you. Head - ing out in my
86
E7(♯5)
E7
Am7(♭5)
D7(♯5)
D7
Repeat to fade
walk - ing shoes town and coun - try rhy - thm and blues.

Valentine Moon

Words and Music by Jools Holland and Sam Brown

10
E♭/G
A♭
B♭7
-bove us young lo - vers we'd meet.
chan - ges we lived our lives well. But the
allumiere toi et moi jeunes amants.
13
E♭/C
E♭/G
A♭
E♭
old town has gone now and it's win - ter too soon. Still
17
E♭/C
E♭/G
A♭6
E♭/B♭
B♭7/D
E♭
(F7)
we waltz be - neath our va - len - tine moon.

Chorus
21
B♭
B♭7/D
E♭
Cm
Va - len - tine moon, va - len - tine moon,
25
B♭
D7/A
Gm
C7
F
we dance to - geth - er as old lo - vers do.
29
B♭
B♭7/A♭
E♭/G
Edim
Va - len - tine moon, va - len - tine moon we
33
B♭/F
B♭/F
Gm7(♭5)
F7/A
B♭
Repeat Verse and Chorus
al - ways re - mem - ber our va - len - tine moon.

What Goes Around

Words and Music by Jools Holland and Sam Brown

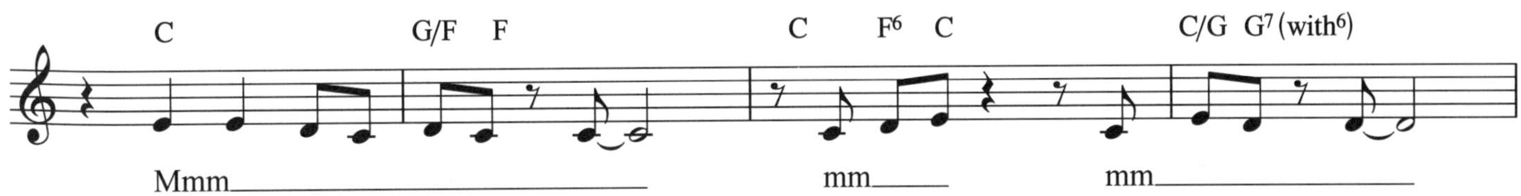
C G/F F C F6 C C/G G7(with6)
Mmm mm mm

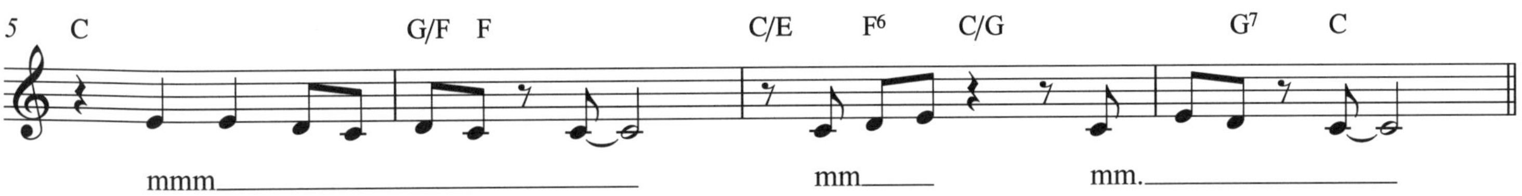
5 C G/F F C/E F6 C/G G7 C
mmm mm mm.

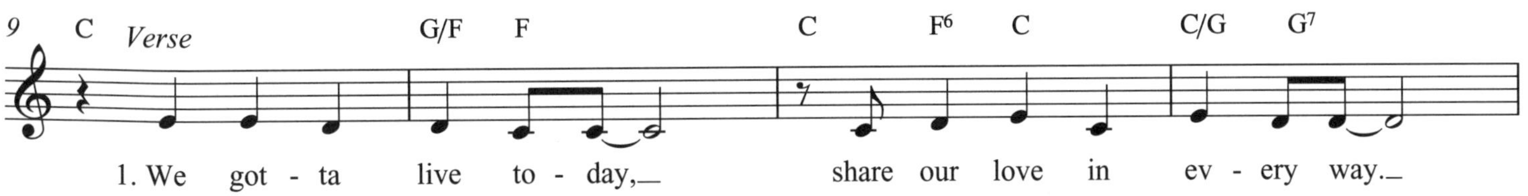
9 C Verse G/F F C F6 C C/G G7
1. We got - ta live to - day, share our love in ev - ery way.

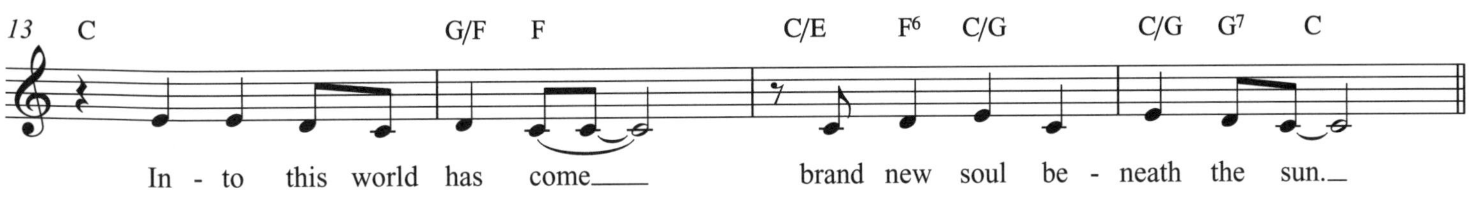
13 C G/F F C/E F6 C/G C/G G7 C
In - to this world has come brand new soul be - neath the sun.

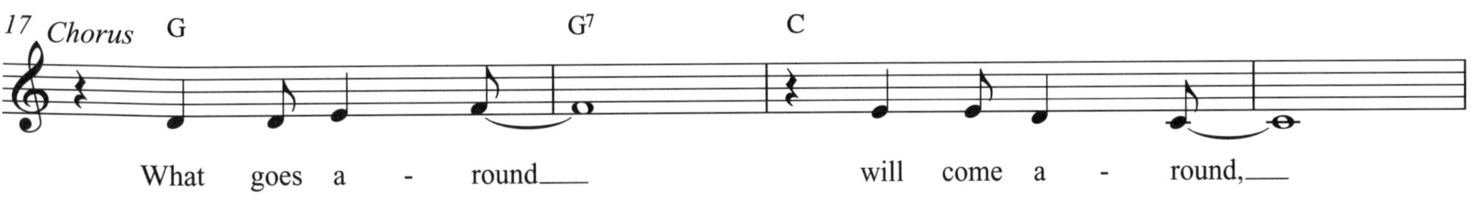
17 Chorus G G7 C
What goes a - round will come a - round,

21 G G7 Am F6 C/E
for it is so you know the young will reap what

24
C/G F6/G C
we have sown.
D♭
Mm
A♭/G♭ G♭
D♭ G♭6 D♭
mm mm
28
A♭7 (with6)
D♭
mm
A♭/G♭ G♭
D♭/F G♭6 D♭/A♭
mm mm
32
A♭7 D♭
D♭
2. Our chil - dren walk a path,
A♭/G♭ G♭
D♭ G♭6 D♭
they will cry and
36
A♭7
they will laugh.
D♭
Through tra - vel they will find
A♭/G♭ G♭
D♭/F G♭6 D♭/A♭
strength of heart and
40
A♭7 D♭
peace of mind.
A♭
What goes a - round
A♭7
D♭
will come a - round,
44
A♭
for it is so
A♭7
you know the young will reap what
B♭m G♭6 D♭/F
48
D♭/A♭ G♭6/A♭ D♭
we have sown.
D
Ohh
A/G G
D/A G6/A D/A
ohh

52
A7 (with6)
D
A/G G
D/F♯ G6 D/A
ohh
ohh.
56
A7 D
D
A/G G
D/A G6/A D/A
3. This much is all we know, you can't take it
60
A7
D
A/G G
D/F♯ G6 D/A
when you go. The love we leave be - hind will live on though
64
A7 D
A
A7
D
we may die. What goes a - round will come a - round,
69
A
A7
Bm G6 D/F♯
D/A G6/A D
for it is so you know the young will reap what we have sown.
73
D
A/G G
D/A G6/A D/A
A7
1. Hmm
2. Ooo
3. Ohh
4. Hey
hmm
ooo
ohhh
hey
Repeat 5 times to fade
77
D
A/G G
D/F♯ G6 D/A
A7 D
hmmm
ooo
ohhh
hey
hmm.
ooo.
ohh.
hey.